Running is Totally for Me

Cassie Celestain

Copyright © 2015 Cassie Celestain

All rights reserved.

ISBN-10: 0-692-50552-0
ISBN-13: 978-0-692-50552-6

DEDICATION

To my fun loving, easy going little girl, Madilynn.
Your unique personality is such a blessing to witness every day! I love you always!

One day Madi was thinking as she made some art
"I really do love this creative part,

but I want to get active and move around.
I will find something and I won't back down!"

Pictures scrolled through her mind of what she could do.

Activities to be done, but what and with who.

She tilted her head tapping in wonder and awe.
Many things to try other than to draw.

Would Madi choose something with balls, movement or courts? All she knew was she wanted to play sports

She would try them with some family and friends.
That way she could test out all the cool trends.

First gymnastics was Madi and Jackson's deal.
She liked doing the backbend and cartwheel.

Together they made moves, yet she could clearly see, "This is fun, but it just *isn't* for me."

Next up with Reagan for a game of basketball. She tried to dribble steady so she wouldn't fall.

Teamwork created points, yet she could clearly see, "This is fun, but it just *isn't* for me."

Then Becker asked Madi to go for a quick swim. She was able to stroke beside him.

United they paddled, yet she could clearly see,
"This is fun, but it just *isn't* for me."

Later with Caley were karate lessons.
She chopped and kicked,
but still had some questions.

Together they practiced, yet she could clearly see, "This is fun, but it just *isn't* for me."

Last Trey invited Madi to play some soccer. She got to be kicker and the blocker.

...he game took much effort, yet she could clearly see,
"This is fun, but it just *isn't* for me."

Wind on her face and the warmth of the sun.
What if she could move forward and just run?

Not wanting to wait longer, she gave it a go.
She pushed herself forward with a smooth flow.

Her arms swung by her side
as her feet touched the ground.
Without a doubt this is the sport she had found!

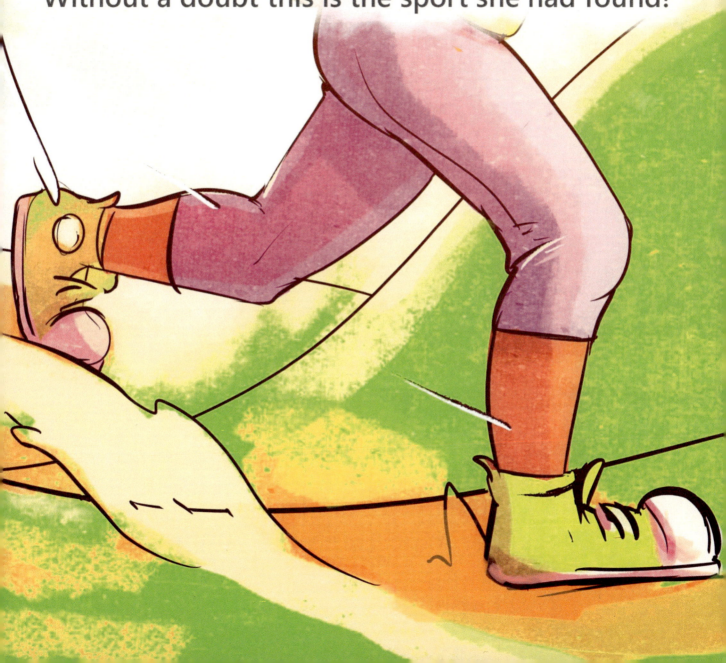

She enjoyed the challenge to keep a faster pace.
Her mind could only think about a race.

t didn't matter much if her friends liked to run.
To her this activity was the best one!

She wanted to keep going. She could clearly see,
"Running is fun and it's **TOTALLY** for me!"

About the Author

Cassie Celestain has a background in Early Childhood Education along with writing for blogs. She lives in Oklahoma with her husband and daughter where running shoes and bike gear can be found in every room of their house. In her spare time she enjoys creating activities for her daughter, reading, crafting and trying new recipes.

About the Vision

Running Is Totally For Me is the first of several books to come. The vision is that when children read the story they will see something in the book that encourages them of possibilities for themselves. The vision goes beyond just these covers though! The plan includes having movement songs and activities to aid the children in discovering themselves through fitness and play.

On the next few pages you will find activities that you can implement with your child(ren) right away. To find more activities and extended information about these included activities visit us at www.TotallyForMe.com.

Activities To Get Moving!

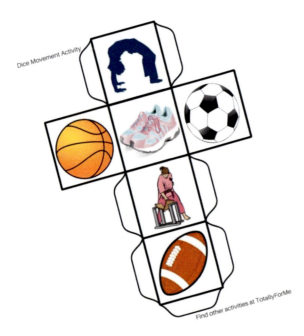

Dice Movement Activity

Prepare: Print the dice template at TotallyForMe.com. Use the blank template to allow your child to draw their own pictures of each activity that was in the book on each side of the dice. Or use the provided template that includes pictures. Cut and tape to create dice.

Play: Have your child roll the dice. They will then make moves with their body that replicates that activity. Ex: Mimic dribbling the ball for basketball. Have the child verbalize what they are doing. If they have trouble knowing what to do guide them with questions to aid them in coming up with a movement.

To get the printables for this activity or find more activities to get your kids moving go to www.TotallyForMe.com!

Verb Actions

Prepare: Review with your child about nouns (people, places, objects) and verbs (action words). Together come up with verbs that they can read that describe movements within the sports from the book. (Ex: jump, hop, spin) Write one word per index card. You can also download the premade verb action cards at TotallyForMe.com.

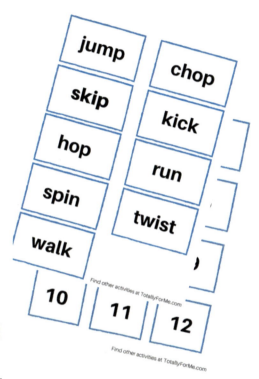

Play: The child draws a card, reads the word and performs the word. If you have two children the game can be set up as a race or a relay for multiple children.

To get the printables for this activity or find more activities to get your kids moving go to www.TotallyForMe.com!

Ball Throw and Measure

Prepare: Gather sports balls, a measuring tape and a writing utensil. Print the activity sheet at TotallyForMe.com.

Play: Mark a standing line. Have the child stand at the standing line and throw each ball. Measure how far each ball is from the start (Older kids can use the measuring tape. Younger kids can measure by steps, their own feet or an object.). Discuss the outcome with your child. Have the child record their answers on the activity sheet.

To get the printables for this activity or find more activities to get your kids moving go to www.TotallyForMe.com!

Made in the USA
Las Vegas, NV
01 March 2024